I0500054

15 LAWS OF FAILURE

Unveiling the Hidden Path to Success

BY:
Joe Martins

Disclaimer:

The information provided in this book, "The 15 Laws of Failure," written by Joe Martins, is intended for general informational purposes only. The author and publisher are not responsible for any actions taken based on the content of this book. Readers should consult professionals or experts in the relevant fields for specific advice related to their individual situations. The author and publisher do not guarantee the accuracy, completeness, or timeliness of the information presented in this book.

TABLE OF CONTENTS

Dedication:

This book is dedicated to all those who have faced failure head-on, yet refused to be defined by it.

To the dreamers who dared to pursue their passions, only to stumble and fall along the way.

To the brave souls who turned their setbacks into stepping stones, using failure as a catalyst for growth and resilience.

To the relentless individuals who never lost sight of their goals, even when the path seemed uncertain and the odds were stacked against them.

To the unwavering spirits who have taught us that success is not measured by the absence of failure, but by the unwavering commitment to rise above it.

This book is for you—the warriors, the trailblazers, the champions of perseverance. May these pages serve as a guiding light, reminding you that failure is not the end, but a crucial part of the journey toward greatness.

May your unwavering spirit and unwavering commitment inspire others to embrace failure as a transformative force and redefine their own path to success.

This is dedicated to you, for showing us the true power that lies within the depths of failure.

Book Description:

Discover the untold secrets to achieving extraordinary success through the art of failure. In "15 Laws of Failure: Unveiling the Hidden Path to Success," embark on a transformative journey that will challenge your perceptions, shift your mindset, and revolutionize your approach to failure.

In this captivating and thought-provoking book, I delve into the treasure trove of 15 laws that unravel the mystique surrounding failure. Prepare to be captivated by stories of resilience, determination, and triumph as you explore the lives of remarkable individuals who turned failure into their greatest ally.

Through real-world case studies and practical examples, you'll witness how the power of resilience propels individuals to soar to new heights, while the art of reflection enables them to extract invaluable lessons from their setbacks. Take a deep dive into the importance of integrity and honoring commitments as a driving force behind long-term success.

This book goes beyond conventional wisdom. It challenges you to redefine success and view failure as a transformative catalyst.

With each chapter, you'll be inspired to cultivate a positive mindset, embrace continuous learning and growth, and take bold action to overcome procrastination.

The insights shared in this book aren't limited to personal achievement—they extend to the realms of business, entrepreneurship, and leadership. Uncover the secrets behind the success of renowned companies and visionary leaders who have harnessed the power of failure to revolutionize industries and leave an indelible mark on the world.

Prepare to embark on a life-changing journey of self-discovery and empowerment. "15 Laws of Failure" will equip you with the tools, strategies, and mindset needed to navigate setbacks, transform failures into stepping stones, and unlock your true potential.

If you're ready to challenge the status quo, embrace failure as a teacher, and rewrite the rules of success, then this book is your roadmap to a future filled with limitless possibilities. Get ready to unveil the hidden path to success like never before

Introduction:

15 Laws of Failure: Unveiling the Hidden Path to Success

In a world that often glorifies success and achievement, it is all too easy to overlook the power and significance of failure. We are bombarded with stories of triumph, where individuals overcome obstacles and rise to the pinnacle of success. But what about those who stumble, fall, and face defeat? Are their stories any less valuable? Can failure truly be a stepping stone to success?

Welcome to "15 Laws of Failure: Unveiling the Hidden Path to Success." In this groundbreaking exploration, I will delve into the often-neglected side of the success narrative—the profound lessons and transformative experiences that emerge from failure. By shining a light on the shadows, I will dig deep to unveil a hidden path, a roadmap to success that traverses through the valleys of setbacks and challenges.

This book is not a collection of tales about overnight successes or easy victories. Instead, it is an illuminating journey that reveals the essential laws that govern failure and its relationship to success. Each chapter delves into a specific law, unraveling its intricacies, and presenting practical examples and case studies to bring these principles to life.

Throughout history, the world's most accomplished individuals have encountered failure on their paths to greatness. From inventors and entrepreneurs to artists and leaders, their stories resonate with resilience, determination, and the unwavering belief in their dreams. I will explore the failures of prominent figures and dissect the lessons they learned along the way. Through their triumphs and tribulations, we will learn the wisdom that failure imparts.

Drawing from a rich tapestry of experiences, I will examine failures in different domains, from business and innovation to personal relationships and self-development. I will discuss the pivotal role of resilience, perseverance, mindset, and integrity in navigating the treacherous terrain of failure. This book will challenge the conventional notions of success and redefine its meaning, incorporating the transformative power of failure into our understanding.

15 Laws of Failure is not solely about theory and abstract concepts. It is a practical guide that empowers you, the reader, to

embark on your own transformative journey. I will provide actionable strategies, exercises, and thought-provoking reflections that allow you to apply the 15 laws of failure to your own life. You will be encouraged to embrace failure, learn from it, and harness its power to propel yourself towards success.

As you turn the pages of "15 Laws of Failure: Unveiling the Hidden Path to Success," prepare to embark on a paradigm-shifting adventure. Open your mind to the possibilities that lie within each setback. Embrace the transformative potential of failure and discover a new way of approaching challenges. You will gain the tools, insights, and mindset necessary to navigate the winding road to success with renewed vigor and resilience.

Remember, dear reader, that failure is not the end—it is merely a stepping stone on the path to greatness. Embrace the 15 laws of failure, and let them guide you towards uncovering your hidden potential, unlocking the doors to success, and embracing a life enriched by the lessons learned through failure.

Are you ready to unveil the hidden path to success? Let us embark on this transformative journey together.

Chapter 1: The Illusion of Perfection: Embracing Imperfections for Growth

I stood on the stage, looking out at the sea of expectant faces. The spotlight illuminated my every move, and the weight of anticipation hung in the air. I had spent countless hours preparing for this moment, honing my skills and perfecting every detail. This was my chance to shine, to show the world what I was capable of. But as I opened my mouth to speak, a wave of anxiety washed over me. What if I made a mistake? What if I wasn't perfect?

The illusion of perfection is a pervasive force in our society. From an early age, we are bombarded with images of flawless beauty, successful careers, and idyllic lifestyles. We are taught to strive for perfection in every aspect of our lives, to hide our flaws and shortcomings at all costs. But the truth is, perfection is an unattainable goal. It is an illusion that keeps us trapped in a cycle of self-doubt and fear.

Take, for example, the United States, a country often seen as a beacon of success and achievement. On the surface, it may appear that everything is perfect – the gleaming skyscrapers, the thriving industries, and the glamorous celebrities. But beneath this facade of perfection lies a different story. Behind closed doors, there are struggles, failures, and imperfections that are rarely acknowledged.

Consider the lives of those who have achieved great success. From inventors to entrepreneurs, their journeys are often paved with failures and setbacks. Thomas Edison, the renowned inventor of the light bulb, famously said, "I have not failed. I've just found 10,000 ways that won't work." It was through embracing his imperfections and learning from his mistakes that he ultimately succeeded.

In the business world, failure is not only inevitable but also essential for growth. Some of the most successful companies today, such as Apple and Microsoft, have faced major setbacks along the way. It was their ability to adapt, learn from their failures, and embrace imperfections that allowed them to thrive.

Beyond the realm of business, the illusion of perfection affects us on a personal level. We strive for the perfect body, the perfect relationship, and the perfect life. We compare ourselves to others, constantly seeking validation and approval. But in doing so, we overlook the beauty and growth that come from embracing our imperfections.

When we let go of the illusion of perfection, we open ourselves up to a world of possibilities. We become more compassionate towards ourselves and others. We give ourselves permission to make mistakes, to learn from them, and to grow. It is through our imperfections that we find our true strength and authenticity.

In the chapters that follow, I will explore the 15 laws of failure, principles that challenge the notion of perfection and encourage a new perspective on failure. These laws will provide practical guidance on how to navigate through setbacks, embrace imperfections, and ultimately find success on your own terms.

So, as I stepped onto the stage that day, I let go of the illusion of perfection. I embraced my imperfections and allowed myself to be vulnerable. And in that moment, something magical happened. The audience connected with me on a deeper level, and my message resonated with them in ways I had never imagined. It was then that I realized the true power of embracing imperfections for growth.

Join me on this journey as we explore the 15 laws of failure and discover the transformative power of embracing imperfections. Together, we will challenge the illusion of perfection and unlock the doors to personal and professional growth.

Chapter 2: The Fear Factor: Conquering Fear and Embracing Risks

I stood at the edge of the towering cliff, my heart pounding in my chest. The wind whipped through my hair, and the sound of crashing waves filled the air. My palms were sweaty, and my legs felt weak. Fear coursed through every fiber of my being, threatening to paralyze me. But deep down, I knew that if I wanted to grow and achieve my goals, I had to conquer this fear and take the leap.

The Fear Factor is the second law of failure, and it is a powerful force that holds us back from reaching our full potential. Fear can manifest itself in many ways – fear of failure, fear of rejection, fear of the unknown. It acts as a barrier, keeping us trapped within our comfort zones and preventing us from taking the necessary risks for growth and success.

In the context of the United States, a country known for its entrepreneurial spirit and innovation, the Fear Factor is particularly prevalent. Many groundbreaking inventions and advancements have been born out of individuals who were willing to take risks and conquer their fears. From the Wright brothers' first flight to the technological revolution of Silicon Valley, these achievements would not have been possible without individuals who embraced risks and overcame their fears.

Consider the story of Elon Musk, the visionary entrepreneur behind companies such as Tesla and SpaceX. Musk has repeatedly faced criticism and skepticism throughout his career. From the electric car industry to space exploration, he has tackled seemingly insurmountable challenges. But what sets Musk apart is his willingness to confront his fears head-on and take calculated risks. Despite facing numerous setbacks and failures, Musk has persevered, driven by his vision and the belief that taking risks is essential for progress.

In our personal lives, the Fear Factor can hinder our growth and limit our experiences. We may dream of starting our own business, pursuing a passion, or making a significant life change. However, the fear of failure or the fear of stepping into the unknown can prevent us from taking that crucial first step.

But what if we were to view fear differently? What if we saw fear as an opportunity for growth, a catalyst for personal development? By reframing our perception of fear, we can transform it into a powerful motivator rather than a paralyzing force.

Conquering fear requires a shift in mindset and a willingness to embrace risks. It means stepping out of our comfort zones and being open to the possibility of failure. Taking calculated risks can lead to unexpected opportunities, personal growth, and even success beyond our wildest dreams.

Think about the entrepreneurs who have launched successful startups or the artists who have shared their work with the world. They had to confront their fears of rejection and failure, taking the leap despite the uncertainty. It was through embracing risks that they were able to achieve their goals and make a lasting impact.

In the chapters that follow, I will explore the 15 laws of failure, including strategies for conquering fear and embracing risks. I will share practical insights and real-life examples that demonstrate the transformative power of facing our fears head-on.

So, as I stood on the edge of that cliff, fear coursing through my veins, I took a deep breath. I reminded myself that growth and success lie on the other side of fear. With each passing moment, my determination grew stronger. And then, with a surge of adrenaline, I took the leap.

Join me on this journey as we explore the 15 laws of failure and learn how to conquer fear, embrace risks, and unlock our true potential. Together, we will confront our fears and discover the extraordinary possibilities that await us on the other side.

Chapter 3: The Power of Resilience: Embracing Failure as a Stepping Stone to Success

I sat in my dimly lit office, surrounded by stacks of rejection letters and unfinished projects. The weight of failure pressed down on me, threatening to crush my spirit. It would have been easy to give up, to succumb to the belief that I was not meant for success. But in that moment of despair, a flicker of resilience ignited within me. I realized that failure was not the end but rather a stepping stone on the path to success.

The Power of Resilience is the third law of failure, and it is a transformative force that allows us to navigate the setbacks and challenges that life throws our way. Resilience is the ability to bounce back from failure, to adapt and learn from our mistakes, and to keep moving forward despite adversity. It is through embracing failure and cultivating resilience that we can ultimately achieve success.

In the context of the United States and other developed nations, resilience has played a significant role in the growth and progress of individuals and societies. Throughout history, we can find countless examples of individuals who faced failure, but through their resilience, went on to achieve remarkable success.

Consider the story of Abraham Lincoln, one of the most revered presidents in American history. Lincoln experienced a series of failures and setbacks, from multiple business failures to electoral defeats. Yet, he did not let these failures define him. Instead, he harnessed the power of resilience, learned from his mistakes, and persisted in his pursuit of leadership. Ultimately, Lincoln's resilience and determination led him to the presidency, where he played a pivotal role in shaping the nation's history.

Resilience is not limited to individuals; it is also crucial for the progress of nations. Developed nations, like the United States, have faced their fair share of failures and challenges throughout history. From economic recessions to natural disasters, these nations have had to rely on resilience to rebuild and move forward. By embracing failure as a stepping stone to success, they have been able to create innovative solutions, foster economic growth, and improve the quality of life for their citizens.

But how can we cultivate resilience in our own lives? How can we shift our mindset and embrace failure as an opportunity for growth?

It starts with changing our perception of failure. Instead of viewing failure as a final outcome or a reflection of our worth, we should see it as a valuable learning experience. Failure provides us with feedback, highlighting areas where we can improve and guiding us towards new approaches. By reframing failure as a stepping stone, we can shift our focus from the negative aspects to the lessons and opportunities it presents.

Practical situations can serve as reminders of the power of resilience. Think about entrepreneurs who faced multiple failed ventures before achieving success. They embraced failure as a natural part of the journey, leveraging their experiences to refine their strategies and ultimately achieve their goals. By recognizing that failure is not a roadblock but a necessary part of the process, they were able to build resilient mindsets that propelled them towards success.

In our personal lives, resilience allows us to bounce back from setbacks and challenges. It enables us to face adversity head-on, adapt to change, and persevere in the pursuit of our dreams. By embracing failure as a teacher rather than an enemy, we gain the strength to overcome obstacles and continue growing.

In the chapters that follow, I will delve deeper into the 15 laws of failure, including strategies for cultivating resilience and embracing failure as a stepping stone to success. Together, we will challenge the traditional perception of failure and develop a new mindset that empowers us to bounce back, learn, and thrive.

To cultivate resilience, we must develop a mindset that embraces challenges and setbacks as opportunities for growth. It involves reframing our thoughts and beliefs about failure, recognizing that it does not define us but rather provides valuable lessons and insights.

One practical way to develop resilience is by adopting a growth mindset. This mindset acknowledges that abilities and skills can be developed through dedication, effort, and learning from mistakes. Instead of seeing failure as a reflection of our inherent abilities, we view it as a chance to improve and progress.

Let's consider the case study of Thomas Edison, the renowned inventor. Edison famously attempted thousands of experiments before successfully inventing the practical electric light bulb. When asked about his failures, he remarked, "I have not failed. I've just found 10,000 ways that won't work." Edison's resilience and unwavering determination propelled him forward, allowing him to turn failure into progress and ultimately achieve groundbreaking success.

In addition to a growth mindset, resilience is fostered through the development of emotional intelligence. Emotional intelligence involves recognizing and managing our emotions, as well as understanding and empathizing with others. By cultivating emotional intelligence, we can better navigate the challenges that come with failure, bounce back more quickly, and maintain a positive outlook.

Furthermore, building a strong support network is essential for resilience. Surrounding ourselves with individuals who uplift and encourage us during challenging times can provide the necessary emotional support and perspective. In the United States and other developed nations, support systems such as mentorship programs, networking events, and professional communities play a crucial role in fostering resilience and helping individuals overcome failures.

Resilience is not limited to personal growth; it also influences the success of organizations and societies. In the face of economic downturns or global crises, resilient nations and businesses adapt and innovate to overcome challenges. By embracing failure as a stepping stone, they identify areas for improvement, implement necessary changes, and emerge stronger than before.

As readers, it is crucial to embrace the power of resilience and undergo a paradigm shift in our mindset towards failure. By understanding that failure is not an endpoint but a stepping stone to success, we can build resilience, adapt to change, and persevere in the pursuit of our goals.

In the chapters that follow, I will further explore additional laws of failure, uncovering insights and strategies to navigate challenges and setbacks. Readers will discover how self-awareness, adaptability, collaboration, continuous learning, and other key principles contribute to our ability to overcome failure and achieve success.

Together, let's embark on this transformative journey, embracing the power of resilience and rewriting our narratives around failure. By doing so, we can unlock our true potential and create a future defined by growth, perseverance, and unwavering resilience.

Chapter 4: The Art of Self-Awareness: Discovering Strengths and Weaknesses

I gazed at my reflection in the mirror, contemplating the person I saw staring back at me. It was a moment of deep introspection, a quest to understand myself on a profound level. This journey of self-discovery is what I refer to as the Art of Self-Awareness: the ability to uncover our strengths and weaknesses. It is through this process that we gain a clearer understanding of who we are and how we can navigate failure more effectively.

The Art of Self-Awareness is the fourth law of failure, and it is a fundamental principle that can lead to a paradigm shift in our mindset towards failure. It is about peeling back the layers, delving into our core essence, and embracing both our strengths and weaknesses as integral parts of our identity.

In the context of the United States and other developed nations, self-awareness plays a pivotal role in personal and professional growth. When individuals and societies are aware of their strengths, they can harness them to achieve extraordinary feats. Likewise, acknowledging weaknesses allows for targeted improvement and development. By understanding our limitations, we can seek support, acquire new skills, or collaborate with others to overcome challenges.

Consider the story of Steve Jobs, the co-founder of Apple Inc. Jobs was known for his visionary leadership and revolutionary products. However, his success was not solely attributed to his strengths. Jobs was acutely aware of his weaknesses and surrounded himself with individuals who complemented his skill set. By acknowledging his limitations, he built a team that was collectively strong, enabling Apple to thrive and innovate.

Practical situations can illuminate the power of self-awareness. Imagine a young entrepreneur who embarks on a business venture without a clear understanding of their strengths and weaknesses. As the challenges and setbacks arise, they may struggle to adapt, lacking the self-awareness necessary to navigate the complexities of entrepreneurship. However, by embarking on a journey of self-discovery, this entrepreneur can identify their areas of expertise and seek guidance or resources to address their weaknesses. The result is a more resilient and adaptable approach to failure, increasing the chances of success.

Self-awareness is not limited to individuals; it is also crucial at the societal level. Developed nations, such as the United States, thrive when they acknowledge their strengths and weaknesses. By leveraging their strengths, such as technological advancements, innovation, or infrastructure, they can position themselves for success. Simultaneously, recognizing weaknesses, such as income inequality or environmental challenges, prompts the development of targeted strategies and policies to address these issues effectively.

To embark on the journey of self-awareness, we must first cultivate a willingness to explore and reflect upon our inner selves. This involves taking the time for introspection, engaging in activities like journaling, meditation, or seeking feedback from trusted mentors and friends. By peeling back the layers, we uncover our passions, values, and unique qualities that set us apart.

Furthermore, embracing a growth mindset is essential in the pursuit of self-awareness. Recognizing that our strengths and weaknesses are not fixed but can be developed and improved over time allows us to approach failures with a sense of curiosity and a commitment to growth..

Together, let us embark on this transformative journey of self-discovery, embracing the Art of Self-Awareness to redefine our perception of failure and unlock our full potential.

Chapter 5: The Importance of Adaptability: Thriving in the Face of Change

I stood at the edge of a vast, snow-covered landscape, observing the magnificent beauty of the Russian wilderness. It was a reminder of the country's resilience and ability to adapt to harsh and ever-changing conditions. This scene embodied the essence of the fifth law of failure: the Importance of Adaptability.

Adaptability is the capacity to adjust, innovate, and thrive in the face of change. It is about embracing uncertainty and proactively responding to new circumstances. In a world where change is inevitable, those who can adapt are more likely to navigate failure successfully and seize opportunities for growth.

To understand the significance of adaptability, let us explore the context of both Russia and developed nations. Russia, with its rich history and diverse geography, has faced numerous challenges throughout its existence. From political and economic upheavals to environmental shifts, the country has demonstrated its adaptability in the face of adversity.

Consider the transition from the Soviet Union to the Russian Federation. Following the dissolution of the Soviet Union, Russia experienced a period of significant change and uncertainty. The country had to adapt its political, economic, and social systems to fit the new realities. While there were undoubtedly challenges and setbacks along the way, Russia's ability to adapt allowed it to navigate the complexities of the transition and emerge as a global power.

Similarly, developed nations have experienced the need for adaptability in various contexts. From technological advancements to economic shifts, these nations must continually adapt to remain competitive and sustain their progress. Take the example of the United States, where industries such as manufacturing have undergone significant changes due to globalization and automation. Those who have embraced adaptability by retraining their workforce, investing in new technologies, and diversifying their economies have fared better than those who resisted change.

Practical situations further illustrate the importance of adaptability. Imagine an entrepreneur who launched a successful business but suddenly faces disruption due to emerging technologies or changing consumer preferences. In this scenario, adaptability becomes the key to survival. By recognizing the need to pivot, embracing innovation, and finding new ways to meet customer needs, the entrepreneur can navigate the challenges and remain competitive.

The paradigm shift required to embrace adaptability lies in viewing change as an opportunity rather than a threat. It is human nature to resist change and seek stability, but this mindset limits our growth and leaves us vulnerable to failure. By shifting our perception and embracing change as a catalyst for innovation and progress, we open ourselves up to new possibilities and increase our chances of success.

Cultivating adaptability requires a combination of mindset and action. It starts with developing a growth mindset, recognizing that change is a natural part of life and presents opportunities for learning and growth. Additionally, building resilience, as discussed in the previous chapter, equips us with the ability to navigate the uncertainties that come with change.

In the chapters that follow, we will explore additional laws of failure, uncovering insights and strategies to enhance our adaptability and thrive in the face of change. By understanding the Importance of Adaptability and cultivating this trait within ourselves, we can transform our mindset of failure and embrace change as a gateway to success.

Together, let us embark on this transformative journey, embracing adaptability as a guiding principle that enables us to navigate failure, seize opportunities, and ultimately thrive in an ever-changing world.

Chapter 6: The Paradox of Control: Letting Go to Gain Control

I found myself standing on the Great Wall of China, marveling at the sheer magnitude of human achievement. As I traced the ancient structure with my gaze, I realized that it embodied a profound lesson: the Paradox of Control. This paradox, the sixth law of failure, reveals that true control comes not from grasping tightly to every aspect of life but from the ability to let go and embrace the uncertainty that failure brings.

The Paradox of Control challenges our conventional understanding of control as the ability to micromanage every detail and ensure a desired outcome. Instead, it teaches us that by relinquishing our tight grip on circumstances, we gain a greater sense of control over our lives and our response to failure.

China, with its rich cultural heritage and rapid development, serves as an apt case study for the Paradox of Control. Over the centuries, China has faced numerous challenges, from political transitions to economic reforms. The nation's ability to adapt and let go of traditional ways of thinking and doing has been key to its remarkable transformation.

Consider China's economic development in recent decades. The country shifted from a centrally planned economy to a market-oriented one, embracing economic reforms and opening up to international trade. This required letting go of strict control over the economy and allowing market forces to play a more significant role. By doing so, China unleashed its economic potential and achieved unprecedented growth.

Similarly, developed nations have encountered situations where the Paradox of Control becomes crucial. Take the example of technological advancements that disrupt established industries. In the face of these disruptions, companies that cling to outdated business models and refuse to adapt often falter. However, those that embrace change, let go of outdated practices, and pivot their strategies gain a renewed sense of control over their future.

Practical situations further illustrate the Paradox of Control. Imagine an individual who meticulously plans every aspect of their life, seeking to control every outcome. However, despite their best efforts, unforeseen events disrupt their plans, leading to frustration and disappointment. In this scenario, the individual's desire for control becomes a hindrance rather than an asset. By letting go of the need for absolute control and embracing the uncertainty of life, they can respond more effectively to failures, adapt to new circumstances, and regain a sense of control over their own growth and happiness.

The paradigm shift required to embrace the Paradox of Control involves recognizing that true control lies in our ability to navigate and respond to failure, rather than in trying to control every external factor. It requires a shift in focus from external circumstances to internal resilience and adaptability. By accepting the fluidity of life, we empower ourselves to make the best choices in the face of failure and to find new paths to success.

One successful individual who embraced the Paradox of Control is Jack Ma, the co-founder of Alibaba Group, one of the world's largest e-commerce companies. Throughout his career, Ma has demonstrated a remarkable ability to let go of control and embrace uncertainty, leading to his tremendous success.

When Alibaba was first founded, it faced numerous challenges and setbacks. Instead of trying to control every aspect of the business, Ma adopted a more adaptive and flexible approach. He empowered his team to take risks, experiment with new ideas, and make decisions independently. By relinquishing the need for absolute control, Ma fostered a culture of innovation and entrepreneurship within Alibaba.

Ma famously said, "Control your destiny by letting go of the illusion of control." He understood that true control comes from empowering others, embracing change, and being open to new possibilities. This mindset allowed Alibaba to navigate the dynamic e-commerce landscape, adapt to evolving customer needs, and expand into various sectors beyond online retail, such as cloud computing, finance, and entertainment.

By embracing the Paradox of Control, Jack Ma transformed Alibaba into a global powerhouse, revolutionizing the e-commerce industry and becoming one of the wealthiest individuals in the world. His ability to let go and embrace uncertainty propelled him to remarkable success, serving as an inspiring example of the power of relinquishing control to gain control.

Jack Ma's journey exemplifies how embracing the Paradox of Control can lead to extraordinary achievements. It demonstrates that by letting go of the illusion of absolute control, we open ourselves up to new opportunities, foster innovation, and gain a greater sense of control over our own growth and success.

Together, let us embark on this transformative journey, embracing the Paradox of Control as a guiding principle that enables us to navigate failure, embrace uncertainty, and ultimately gain a greater sense of control over our lives.

Chapter 7: The Value of Collaboration: Leveraging Networks for Success

As I sat in a bustling coffee shop, I couldn't help but notice the collective energy and synergy that filled the air. It reminded me of the profound truth embedded in the seventh law of failure: the Value of Collaboration. Collaboration, the ability to work together and leverage networks for success, holds the key to unlocking new opportunities and overcoming failure.

In today's interconnected world, no success is achieved in isolation. Collaboration empowers individuals and organizations to tap into a vast pool of knowledge, skills, and resources that they may not possess individually. By harnessing the power of collaboration, we can amplify our strengths, mitigate our weaknesses, and achieve collective success.

To understand the significance of collaboration, let us explore the context of both the United States and the United Kingdom. These nations have a long history of leveraging collaboration to drive innovation, economic growth, and societal progress.

The United States, renowned for its entrepreneurial spirit, has fostered a culture of collaboration that has fueled its success. Silicon Valley, a hub of technological innovation, thrives on collaboration among startups, venture capitalists, universities, and research institutions. This ecosystem of collaboration has given rise to breakthrough technologies, disruptive business models, and transformative ideas.

Similarly, the United Kingdom has a rich tradition of collaboration and partnerships across industries. From academia to industry, collaborations have been instrumental in driving advancements in fields such as healthcare, technology, and creative arts. For example, the collaboration between universities, research institutions, and pharmaceutical companies has led to significant breakthroughs in medical research and the development of life-saving treatments.

Practical situations further illustrate the Value of Collaboration. Consider a scenario where an entrepreneur with a groundbreaking idea lacks the necessary resources and expertise to bring it to fruition. By reaching out to potential collaborators, such as industry experts, investors, or fellow entrepreneurs, they can tap into a network that can provide the knowledge, funding, and support needed to turn their vision into a reality. Collaboration not only expands the entrepreneur's capabilities but also increases their chances of success.

The paradigm shift required to embrace the Value of Collaboration lies in recognizing that success is not a solitary pursuit. Rather than viewing others as competitors, we must see them as potential collaborators and partners. By actively seeking out opportunities for collaboration, we can tap into diverse perspectives, gain access to new resources, and create synergistic outcomes that surpass what we could achieve alone.

One notable individual who exemplifies the power of collaboration is Elon Musk, the CEO of Tesla, SpaceX, and several other innovative companies. Musk recognizes the value of collaboration in achieving his ambitious goals of revolutionizing the automotive and aerospace industries. He has forged strategic partnerships with other companies, such as NASA and various suppliers, to leverage their expertise and resources. Through collaboration, Musk has been able to accelerate the development of electric vehicles and space exploration, pushing the boundaries of what was once deemed impossible.

Another remarkable example is the collaboration between Apple and IBM. In 2014, these two tech giants joined forces to bring together Apple's user-friendly devices and IBM's expertise in enterprise solutions. This collaboration resulted in a powerful partnership that transformed how businesses utilize mobile technology and enhanced productivity in various industries. By leveraging each other's strengths and networks, Apple and IBM created a synergy that led to significant advancements in enterprise mobility.

These examples highlight how collaboration has been instrumental in the success of individuals and companies. By seeking out partnerships, sharing knowledge, and pooling resources, they were able to tap into collective intelligence, drive innovation, and achieve remarkable outcomes that would have been challenging or impossible to accomplish alone.

The experiences of these successful individuals and companies demonstrate the paradigm shift required to embrace the Value of

Collaboration. It involves recognizing that collaboration is not a sign of weakness or dependency but rather a strategic approach that amplifies capabilities, expands networks, and drives collective success. By embracing collaboration, we can break down silos, foster innovation, and create a thriving ecosystem where everyone benefits.

As we continue our exploration of the 15 laws of failure, the Value of Collaboration serves as a guiding principle that can transform our mindset and reshape our approach to failure. By embracing collaboration, we can unlock new opportunities, overcome challenges, and harness the power of networks to achieve success beyond our individual capabilities.

Together, let us embark on this transformative journey, valuing collaboration as a guiding principle that enables us to navigate failure, seize opportunities, and collectively thrive in an interconnected world.

Chapter 8: The Path to Mastery: Embracing Continuous Learning and Growth

As I sat in a quiet corner of the library, surrounded by rows of books representing centuries of accumulated knowledge, I was struck by the profound truth embedded in the eighth law of failure: the Path to Mastery. Mastery is not a destination but a lifelong journey of continuous learning and growth. It is the relentless pursuit of improvement, the unwavering commitment to honing our skills and expanding our knowledge.

In today's rapidly evolving world, where change is constant and innovation is the key to success, embracing continuous learning and growth is more critical than ever. The United States and the United Kingdom, renowned for their contributions to science, technology, and the arts, serve as exceptional case studies of nations that have embraced the Path to Mastery.

In the United States, we witness the power of continuous learning and growth in the realm of technology. Companies like Google, Apple, and Microsoft, which have revolutionized our digital landscape, prioritize a culture of learning. They provide their employees with opportunities for professional development, encourage experimentation, and foster an environment where mistakes are seen as learning opportunities. By continuously updating their skills and staying at the forefront of technological advancements, these companies have achieved unprecedented success and shaped the future.

Similarly, the United Kingdom boasts a rich tradition of academic excellence and innovation. Renowned educational institutions like Oxford and Cambridge have long been bastions of knowledge and intellectual pursuits. By nurturing a culture of lifelong learning and investing in research and development, the UK has become a global hub for innovation and scientific breakthroughs. The success of British scientists, inventors, and artists is a testament to their commitment to continuous growth and the pursuit of mastery.

Practical situations further illustrate the importance of the Path to Mastery. Consider an entrepreneur who founded a successful startup but faces the challenge of scaling the business. By embracing continuous learning, the entrepreneur seeks out mentors, attends industry conferences, and avidly reads books and articles to acquire new skills and knowledge. Through this dedication to growth, they acquire the necessary expertise in areas such as marketing, finance, and team management, enabling them to navigate challenges and propel their business to new heights.

The paradigm shift required to embrace the Path to Mastery lies in understanding that failure is not an endpoint but a stepping stone on the journey to mastery. It is through failure that we learn, adapt, and improve. Embracing continuous learning and growth means viewing failure as an opportunity to refine our skills, gain new insights, and pivot our strategies.

As we embark on the Path to Mastery, we must foster a growth mindset that embraces challenges, seeks feedback, and values persistence. By cultivating a passion for learning and a commitment to growth, we can transcend the limitations of failure and unlock our full potential.

Cristiano Ronaldo: One of the greatest footballers of all time, Ronaldo's relentless pursuit of mastery is evident throughout his career. Despite achieving numerous accolades and records, he maintains a hunger for improvement. Ronaldo is known for his rigorous training regimen, commitment to physical fitness, and dedication to refining his skills. He constantly seeks feedback from coaches, studies opponents to identify weaknesses, and continuously adapts his game to stay at the top of his field. By embracing continuous learning and growth, Ronaldo has consistently evolved as a player and maintained his exceptional performance over the years.

Serena Williams: A legendary tennis player, Serena Williams epitomizes the concept of continuous learning and growth. Despite already being considered one of the greatest athletes in her sport, Williams continues to seek ways to improve and expand her game. She embraces new training techniques, works with coaches to refine her technique, and actively seeks out opportunities to learn from her competitors. By consistently pushing herself and embracing a growth mindset, Williams has achieved remarkable success and cemented her legacy as one of the greatest tennis players of all time.

LeBron James: As one of the most dominant basketball players in history, LeBron James exemplifies the Path to Mastery through his commitment to continuous learning and growth. Despite his immense talent, James constantly seeks ways to improve his game. He studies film, analyzes opponents' strategies, and works tirelessly on developing new skills and refining existing ones. James also actively seeks mentorship and guidance from coaches and veteran players, recognizing that there is always more to learn. This dedication to mastery has allowed him to remain at the forefront of the sport for over a decade.

These examples from the world of sports demonstrate how embracing continuous learning and growth is a vital aspect of achieving mastery. By continuously honing their skills, seeking feedback, and adapting to changing circumstances, these athletes have maintained their peak performance and achieved extraordinary success. They serve as inspiring role models for individuals seeking to apply the Path to Mastery in their own lives and careers.

By following in the footsteps of these athletes, we can understand that the pursuit of mastery requires an unwavering commitment to improvement, a thirst for knowledge, and a willingness to step outside our comfort zones. As we embark on our own journey of continuous learning and growth, we can unlock our potential, overcome failure, and strive for greatness in all aspects of life.

Together, let us embrace the power of continuous learning, unleash our potential, and chart our course to mastery in the face of failure and beyond.

Chapter 9: The Art of Reflection: Extracting Lessons from Failure

As I sat in contemplation, the weight of past failures pressing upon me, I realized that failure alone does not define our journey. It is through the transformative power of reflection that failure becomes a profound teacher, guiding us toward growth and resilience. Welcome to the ninth law of failure: the Art of Reflection—Extracting Lessons from Failure.

Reflection is not merely dwelling on the past or wallowing in regret. It is a deliberate and introspective process that allows us to extract valuable insights and wisdom from our failures. Through reflection, we shift our focus from the disappointment of failure to the hidden gems of knowledge that lie within.

To illuminate the path of the Art of Reflection, let us turn our attention to two remarkable countries: Spain and France. Both nations have faced significant challenges throughout their histories, yet they have risen above adversity by embracing the art of reflection.

In Spain, the economic crisis of 2008 left a profound impact on the nation. Instead of succumbing to despair, Spain's leaders and citizens engaged in deep reflection, seeking to understand the underlying causes and identify necessary changes. This period of introspection led to reforms in the financial sector, a renewed focus on innovation and entrepreneurship, and an emphasis on sustainable economic growth. By extracting lessons from the crisis, Spain emerged stronger, more resilient, and better equipped to navigate future challenges.

Similarly, France has experienced its share of setbacks and failures. One notable example is their approach to education reform. Over the years, French policymakers have engaged in reflection and introspection, analyzing the strengths and weaknesses of their educational system. They have sought to learn from their failures, adapt their strategies, and implement reforms that address shortcomings. Through reflection, France has made significant advancements in education, fostering a system that promotes innovation, creativity, and excellence.

Practical situations further exemplify the importance of the Art of Reflection. Imagine an entrepreneur who launched a startup that ultimately failed. Instead of giving in to discouragement, they take the time to reflect on their experiences. They identify the factors that contributed to the failure, such as inadequate market research or flawed product development. Through this introspection, they extract valuable lessons that inform their next venture. Armed with newfound knowledge, they are better prepared to navigate challenges and increase their chances of success.

The paradigm shift required to embrace the Art of Reflection lies in understanding that failure is not a dead-end, but rather a catalyst for growth. By approaching failure with a reflective mindset, we transcend the notion of defeat and instead view it as an opportunity for personal and professional development. Reflection allows us to learn from our mistakes, refine our strategies, and chart a more successful course moving forward.

Here are a few examples of successful individuals from different fields who have embraced the Art of Reflection to extract lessons from failure and achieve remarkable success:

Usain Bolt: The Jamaican sprinter Usain Bolt, widely regarded as one of the greatest sprinters of all time, has faced setbacks and failures throughout his career. However, he has always approached these challenges with a reflective mindset. By analyzing his races, identifying areas for improvement, and making necessary adjustments, Bolt continuously refined his technique and became an Olympic champion, setting world records in the process.

Oprah Winfrey: A media mogul and philanthropist, Oprah Winfrey has faced numerous challenges and setbacks throughout her life. However, she has always approached failure as an opportunity for growth and reflection. By extracting lessons from her own experiences, Winfrey has become an influential figure in the entertainment industry and an inspiration to millions worldwide.

J.K. Rowling: The author of the Harry Potter series, J.K. Rowling faced multiple rejections before finding success. However, she used these setbacks as an opportunity to reflect on her writing and storytelling skills. Through introspection and continuous improvement, she transformed her failures into the foundation of a global literary phenomenon.

Lionel Messi: The Argentine footballer Lionel Messi has achieved extraordinary success on the football field. However, he has also faced disappointments and failures along the way. Messi's ability to reflect on his performances, understand his mistakes, and work on improving his skills has played a crucial role in his development as a player. By extracting lessons from failure, Messi has become a record-breaking goal scorer and a legend of the sport.

Serena Williams: As mentioned earlier, Serena Williams, one of the most accomplished tennis players of all time, embraces the Art of Reflection to continuously improve her game. By analyzing her matches, reflecting on her performance, and identifying areas for growth, Williams has been able to adapt her strategies and maintain her dominance in women's tennis.

Mo Farah: The British long-distance runner Mo Farah has faced numerous obstacles and failures throughout his career. However, he never let setbacks define him. Instead, Farah used these experiences as opportunities for reflection and growth. By analyzing his races, strategizing, and making adjustments, he transformed himself into a multiple Olympic and World

Champion, solidifying his status as one of the most successful long-distance runners in history.

These individuals from diverse fields demonstrate the transformative power of reflection in achieving success. They serve as shining examples of how learning from failure, extracting lessons, and making necessary adjustments can lead to remarkable achievements. By following in their footsteps, we can navigate our own journeys with a reflective mindset, embrace growth, and unlock our true potential.

Remember, the Art of Reflection is not limited to any particular domain but is applicable to all aspects of life. Whether you are an entrepreneur, artist, athlete, or professional, the ability to extract lessons from failure through reflection is a fundamental skill that can propel you towards your goals and aspirations.

Together, let us embark on the transformative journey of reflection, extracting lessons from failure and emerging stronger, wiser, and more determined to fulfill our potential

Chapter 10: The Perils of Procrastination: Taking Action to Overcome Failure

In the realm of success and achievement, one of the most dangerous pitfalls we often encounter is the perils of procrastination. Procrastination is the act of delaying or postponing tasks and actions that need to be completed. It can be tempting to put off important actions, whether due to fear, uncertainty, or a lack of motivation. However, the consequences of succumbing to procrastination can be detrimental to our goals, dreams, and ultimately, our journey to success.

When we procrastinate, we create a self-imposed barrier between ourselves and our aspirations. The longer we delay taking action, the greater the likelihood of failure becomes. Each moment spent procrastinating is a moment wasted, where opportunities pass us by and the path to success becomes increasingly elusive. By succumbing to the perils of procrastination, we willingly surrender our control over our own destiny.

Imagine standing on the edge of a diving board, ready to plunge into the crystal-clear waters below. The exhilaration and excitement of taking the leap fill your heart, but fear and doubt start to creep in. You hesitate, unable to take that crucial step forward. You may find yourself clinging to the safety of the familiar, avoiding the unknown, and choosing momentary comfort over long-term growth.

Dubai, the United Arab Emirates, and Singapore are two shining examples of nations that have recognized the perils of procrastination and taken bold action to overcome failure. Both have transformed themselves from relatively small and underdeveloped territories into economic powerhouses through forward-thinking strategies and proactive decision-making. They have embraced the mindset of taking action, even in the face of uncertainty, and have reaped the rewards of their proactive approach.

Dubai's transformation from a desert city to a global hub of commerce, tourism, and innovation is a testament to the power of action. The city's leaders recognized the need to diversify its economy, invest in infrastructure, and attract international businesses and tourists. By boldly taking action, Dubai has become a symbol of ambition, progress, and success.

Similarly, Singapore's journey from a small trading port to a thriving metropolis showcases the perils of procrastination and the importance of decisive action. Singapore's leaders understood the risks of complacency and embraced a culture of constant adaptation and innovation. Through strategic planning, investments in education and technology, and a focus on attracting global talent, Singapore has become a beacon of economic prosperity and excellence.

By examining these real-life examples, we can draw inspiration and learn valuable lessons about the perils of procrastination. Inaction and delaying action not only hinder our progress but also rob us of the opportunity to learn, grow, and achieve our full potential.

It is essential to recognize that taking action does not guarantee immediate success or eliminate the possibility of failure. However, by taking proactive steps towards our goals, we position ourselves for growth, learning, and increased resilience in the face of challenges. Each action we take, no matter how small, propels us forward and brings us closer to our desired outcomes.

In the next chapters, we will delve deeper into the remaining laws of failure, each designed to shift our mindset, challenge our perceptions, and ignite the transformative power within us. Together, these laws will empower us to overcome the perils of procrastination, embrace action, and embark on a path of growth, achievement, and lasting success.

Here are a few examples of successful individuals, companies and businesses who have applied the law of taking action to overcome failure:

Zoom: The video conferencing platform Zoom experienced tremendous success in recent years, especially during the global pandemic. The company took swift action to meet the increased demand for remote communication and collaboration tools. By quickly adapting their technology and providing reliable and user-friendly solutions, Zoom became an essential tool for businesses, organizations, and individuals worldwide

Nike: The multinational sportswear giant Nike has a long history of taking action to overcome failure. One notable example is their "Just Do It" campaign, which encourages individuals to step out of their comfort zones and take action toward their goals. By embracing this philosophy, Nike has not only built a successful brand but has also inspired countless athletes and individuals to push their limits and achieve greatness.

Simone Biles: The Olympic gymnast, Simone Biles, exemplifies the power of taking action to overcome failure. She faced numerous challenges throughout her career, including setbacks and injuries. However, by consistently pushing herself to take action, persistently practicing, and continually striving for improvement, she has become one of the most decorated gymnasts in history and an inspiration to many.

These recent success stories demonstrate the transformative power of taking action to overcome failure. By emulating the mindset and actions of these individuals and businesses, we can break free from the perils of procrastination and unlock our own potential for success.

By incorporating the lessons and mindset of these successful individuals and businesses into our own lives, we can overcome the perils of procrastination, ignite our inner drive, and unlock our true potential.

Chapter 11: The Busy Law: Having Reasons to Fail

In this chapter, I will explore the concept of the Busy Law, which revolves around having reasons to fail. It is a law that stems from the tendency to fill our lives with busyness and excuses, ultimately hindering our progress and leading to failure. As we delve into this thought-provoking topic, we will examine practical situations and stories of individuals and developed nations, shedding light on how the Busy Law can impact our lives and how we can overcome it.

The Illusion of Busyness:

In today's fast-paced world, it is common for many of us to wear busyness as a badge of honor. We fill our schedules to the brim, constantly rushing from one task to another, and convince ourselves that we are productive. However, buried beneath this illusion of busyness lies the real danger—the subconscious desire to have reasons to fail. By keeping ourselves occupied with trivial tasks or avoiding taking action on important goals, we create a shield of busyness that shields us from confronting our fears and pursuing our dreams.

The Comfort of Excuses:

Excuses become the ammunition we use to justify our lack of progress or success. We tell ourselves that we don't have enough time, resources, or abilities to achieve what we truly desire. These self-imposed limitations create a false sense of comfort, shielding us from the discomfort and uncertainty that come with stepping out of our comfort zones. However, this comfort is deceptive, for it traps us in a cycle of mediocrity and perpetuates our failure.

Practical Situations and Case Studies:

Let's consider the story of Sarah, a talented artist who dreams of showcasing her work to the world. Despite her passion and skill, she finds herself caught in the Busy Law. She fills her days with menial tasks, convincing herself that she doesn't have enough time or resources to pursue her artistic endeavors. By succumbing to the Busy Law, Sarah denies herself the opportunity to fulfill her potential and share her creativity with others.

In a broader context, we can observe how the Busy Law impacts the progress of developed nations. Some countries may fall into the trap of being preoccupied with maintaining the status quo rather than embracing innovative ideas and investing in their future. They may become complacent, resting on past achievements and failing to adapt to changing global dynamics. By succumbing to the Busy Law, these nations hinder their own growth and risk falling behind in the global landscape.

Overcoming the Busy Law:

To break free from the Busy Law and create a paradigm shift in our mindset of failure, we must confront our excuses head-on and prioritize our goals and aspirations. It requires a willingness to step out of our comfort zones and challenge the busyness that masks our true potential. By practicing self-awareness, focusing on what truly matters, and making deliberate choices, we can reclaim our time, energy, and resources to invest in our personal and professional growth.

Conclusion:

The Busy Law: Having Reasons to Fail is a powerful concept that urges us to examine the excuses and busyness that hold us back from achieving our goals. By recognizing the illusion of busyness and the comfort of excuses, we can reclaim control over our lives and pursue success with renewed determination. Let us embrace this law and break free from the constraints that hinder our progress, thus opening the doors to a future filled with achievement, growth, and fulfillment.

Chapter 12: The Power of Persistence: Persevering in the Face of Failure

As I sat in my study, contemplating the twelfth law of failure, the Power of Persistence, I couldn't help but feel the weight of its significance. In my own journey as an author and entrepreneur, I have witnessed firsthand the incredible power of persistence in overcoming obstacles and achieving success. It is a concept that transcends time and place, and its impact can be seen in the stories of successful leaders and thriving business hubs around the world.

Consider the inspiring tale of Nelson Mandela, the former President of South Africa. Throughout his life, Mandela faced tremendous adversity, including 27 years of imprisonment for his fight against apartheid. Yet, he never wavered in his belief in the power of persistence and the pursuit of justice. Mandela's unwavering determination and refusal to give up ultimately led to the dismantling of apartheid and the establishment of a democratic South Africa.

Turning our attention to the bustling city-state of Singapore, we find an exemplary business hub that has harnessed the power of persistence to transform itself into a global economic powerhouse. From humble beginnings as a small trading port, Singapore faced numerous challenges and setbacks. However, through visionary leadership and a relentless focus on innovation and adaptability, the nation persevered and became one of the world's leading financial and technological hubs.

In the realm of business, we find the remarkable story of Jack Ma, the founder of Alibaba Group, one of the world's largest e-commerce companies. Ma encountered numerous rejections and failures before achieving success. He faced setbacks, financial struggles, and even a failed attempt to secure employment at KFC. But through his unwavering persistence and belief in his vision, Ma built Alibaba into a global powerhouse, revolutionizing the e-commerce industry and inspiring countless entrepreneurs around the world.

These stories of leaders and thriving business hubs illustrate the transformative power of persistence. They remind us that failure is not a final destination but a stepping stone on the path to success. It is through persistence that we find the strength to navigate through challenging times, learn from our mistakes, and adapt our strategies. The leaders and business hubs that embody the power of persistence inspire us to persevere in the face of failure, to embrace setbacks as opportunities for growth, and to never lose sight of our ultimate goals.

Let us embark on this transformative journey together, as we embrace the power of persistence and chart our course towards a future filled with triumph and fulfillment.

Chapter 13: The Mindset of Success: Cultivating a Positive Attitude

As I embark on this remarkable exploration of the 15 laws of failure, I am captivated by the profound influence of the thirteenth law: the Mindset of Success. This law holds the transformative power to reshape our perception of failure and guide us toward a path of triumph. With an unwavering belief in our abilities and an optimistic outlook, we can cultivate a positive mindset that propels us forward, even in the face of adversity.

Imagine standing on the edge of a precipice, gazing out at the vast horizon before you. It is in this limitless expanse that the power of a positive mindset comes to life. It is a mindset that not only empowers us to embrace failure as a stepping stone to success but also instills in us an unyielding determination to overcome any obstacles that come our way.

To understand the impact of a positive mindset, let us turn our attention to another extraordinary individual whose story epitomizes the power of unwavering optimism and resilience. Meet Serena Williams, the iconic tennis champion known for her indomitable spirit and unparalleled success on the court. Throughout her career, Serena has faced numerous setbacks and challenges, including injuries, personal struggles, and defeats. However, her unwavering belief in herself and her ability to rise above failure has been a driving force behind her continued success. With every setback, she has found the strength to bounce back, learning valuable lessons and using them as fuel for her growth. Serena's story serves as a testament to the transformative power of a positive mindset in the pursuit of greatness.

The United States, a nation built on innovation and perseverance, offers a compelling case study for the impact of a positive mindset on success. From the early pioneers who braved unknown territories to the entrepreneurs who revolutionized industries, the American spirit of optimism and resilience has been instrumental in overcoming failure and achieving remarkable feats. It is this collective mindset that has propelled the nation forward, fostering a culture of innovation and embracing failure as an opportunity for growth.

But cultivating a positive mindset is not confined to individuals alone; it permeates the fabric of developed nations. Consider the success story of Singapore, a small but mighty nation that has transformed itself into a global economic powerhouse. Through visionary leadership and a collective belief in the power of a positive mindset, Singapore has defied the odds and risen above its limitations. The nation's unwavering commitment to cultivating an environment of optimism, innovation, and continuous growth has propelled it to unparalleled success in various sectors.

So, how can we cultivate a positive mindset amidst the challenges and uncertainties of life? It begins with a conscious choice to shift our perspective, embracing failure as a natural part of the journey toward success. By reframing setbacks as opportunities for learning and growth, we can maintain an unwavering belief in our abilities and nurture a positive mindset. Engaging in self-reflection, practicing gratitude, and surrounding ourselves with uplifting influences can further reinforce this transformative mindset.

As we progress through the remaining chapters of this book, we will be exposed to practical strategies and techniques for cultivating a positive mindset. I will delve into the power of affirmations, visualization, and mindfulness practices that empower us to stay resilient and focused on our goals. Together, we will embark on a journey of self-discovery and empowerment, unlocking the true potential within us and redefining our perception of failure.

Let us embrace the Mindset of Success, for within its realm lies the key to unlocking our unlimited potential. By cultivating a positive attitude and reshaping our narrative around failure, we can transcend limitations, surpass expectations, and embark on a path of remarkable achievement. Join me as we navigate the transformative power of a positive mindset and rewrite our stories of failure into tales of triumph.

Chapter 14: The Importance of Integrity: Honoring Commitments for Success

As I embark on this exhilarating exploration of the 15 laws of failure, I am immediately captivated by the resounding significance of the fourteenth law: the Importance of Integrity. It is a profound principle that transcends cultures and generations, guiding us towards a path of honor and accomplishment. In a world where success is often measured by external achievements, integrity serves as the bedrock for true and lasting fulfillment.

Integrity encompasses more than mere honesty and ethical behavior. It is a holistic concept that encompasses consistency, trustworthiness, and a steadfast commitment to honoring our word. When we possess integrity, we become individuals who can be relied upon, whose actions align with their values, and whose commitments are upheld with unwavering dedication.

Consider the United States, a nation known for its exceptional achievements and entrepreneurial spirit. Throughout its history, integrity has played a pivotal role in shaping the success of the nation. From the framers of the Constitution, who crafted a vision of equality and justice, to the innovators and pioneers who built industries and propelled the nation forward, integrity has been a driving force behind their accomplishments. The United States serves as a compelling case study, illustrating the transformative power of integrity in building a strong foundation for success.

In the realm of business and leadership, integrity becomes even more crucial. Imagine a CEO who prioritizes short-term gains over the long-term well-being of their company, making promises they have no intention of keeping or manipulating information to suit their agenda. Such actions erode trust, create a toxic culture, and ultimately lead to failure. Conversely, leaders who embody integrity, who lead with transparency and ethical decision-making, inspire trust and loyalty, fostering an environment of collaboration and success.

Integrity is not limited to grand gestures or public acts of virtue. It resides within the fabric of our daily lives, in the small commitments we make and the promises we honor. It is about being accountable to ourselves and others, staying true to our values, and demonstrating consistency in our actions.

By embracing the importance of integrity and honoring our commitments, we undergo a profound paradigm shift in our mindset of failure. We recognize that success is not solely measured by external accolades but also by the integrity with which we navigate our journey. Integrity becomes a compass, guiding us through challenges and setbacks, and ultimately leading us to a place of personal and professional fulfillment.

As we continue our exploration of the remaining laws of failure, let us remember the transformative power of integrity. It is a force that can change our perceptions, reshape our approach to failure, and ignite a profound shift in our mindset. By embracing integrity and honoring our commitments, we lay the groundwork for a future where success is measured not only by what we achieve but also by the principles and values that underpin our actions.

Join me on this transformative journey to navigate the transformative power of integrity and discover the boundless potential that lies within us when we honor our commitments and embrace the Importance of Integrity.

Chapter 15: The Transformational Power of Failure: Redefining Success

As I delve into the depths of the 15 laws of failure, I am exhilarated to explore the profound concept of the fifteenth law: the Transformational Power of Failure. Brace yourself, dear reader, for we are about to embark on a journey that will shatter your preconceived notions and redefine your understanding of success.

Failure, in its raw and unfiltered form, has long been regarded as a stumbling block, an obstacle to be avoided at all costs. Society has conditioned us to fear failure, to equate it with defeat and disappointment. But what if, just for a moment, we dared to challenge this conventional wisdom? What if, instead of fearing failure, we saw it as a catalyst for growth and transformation?

In the United States, a nation built upon the tenets of resilience and perseverance, countless success stories bear witness to the transformative power of failure. From Thomas Edison, who famously said, "I have not failed. I've just found 10,000 ways that won't work," to the visionary entrepreneurs of Silicon Valley who thrive on the ethos of "failing fast and failing forward," failure has become a stepping stone towards innovation and breakthrough.

But it is not just in the realm of entrepreneurship that failure holds its transformative might. In the development of any developed nation, failure has played a pivotal role in shaping progress. Consider the ingenuity of the Wright brothers, whose repeated failures ultimately led to the invention of the airplane, forever changing the course of human history. Or reflect upon the medical advancements that have emerged from failures in the laboratory, leading to groundbreaking discoveries and life-saving treatments.

The transformational power of failure lies in our ability to extract valuable lessons from our setbacks and use them as stepping stones towards future success. Failure presents us with an opportunity for introspection, forcing us to reevaluate our approaches, refine our strategies, and cultivate resilience. It teaches us perseverance, grit, and the art of bouncing back stronger than ever before.

Redefining success becomes the inevitable consequence of embracing the transformational power of failure. No longer confined to external markers of achievement, success takes on a more profound meaning—a holistic reflection of personal growth, resilience, and the willingness to learn from our missteps. It becomes a journey rather than a destination, a continuous process of self-improvement and self-discovery.

Dear reader, as we conclude this exploration of the 15 laws of failure, I implore you to embrace the transformational power of failure. Shift your perception, dismantle the fear, and dare to redefine success on your own terms. Embrace failure as a catalyst for growth, a necessary ingredient in the recipe of triumph. Let it fuel your determination, ignite your creativity, and propel you towards heights unimagined.

Together, let us embark on this paradigm-shifting journey, where failure becomes the catalyst for our transformation, and success takes on a whole new meaning. May the transformative power of failure awaken within you a profound shift, as you chart a course towards a future defined not by the fear of failure, but by the boundless potential that lies within each setback. The journey awaits, and the power to redefine success is within your grasp.

Summary:

"15 Laws of Failure: Unveiling the Hidden Path to Success" is an enlightening and transformative exploration of failure's profound role in achieving success. In this groundbreaking book, I uncover the 15 essential laws that govern failure, drawing from the experiences of prominent individuals and practical case studies. By examining the power of resilience, perseverance, mindset, and integrity, readers are encouraged to embrace failure as a stepping stone to greatness. With actionable strategies and thought-provoking reflections, this book provides a roadmap for navigating challenges, redefining success, and unleashing one's hidden potential. It is a guide that empowers readers to embrace failure, learn from it, and harness its transformative power to achieve success in all aspects of life.